Foreword

By Jo Bailey Wells, Bishop of Dor

> 'Tell me, what is it you plan to do
> With your one wild and precious life?'
> **'The Summer Day', Mary Oliver**

I shall never finish answering this question, because every day presents challenge and opportunity which call for some adjustment (or at least tweaking) of whatever plan I held. At least for me, that's the way life retains its wild and precious character, its flexibility and grace.

Our lives are wild and precious precisely because they are given and chosen by God. In the light of this truth, the question is not so much one for me to answer as to seek God for an answer. Because, despite the way it usually feels, finding and following my calling doesn't start with me, but with God. As Jesus tells his disciples, 'You did not choose me but I chose you... go and bear fruit, fruit that will last' (John 15.16).

God does have a plan for each of our lives. Of course, because God designed them. It's not an obligatory plan – God will be there even if you don't follow it. But it is the best, a plan for your flourishing and 'fruitfulness'. It's not the kind – like a blueprint – from which you fail if you err or stray. Rather it's a rolling plan that meets you where you are and evolves as your wild and precious life unfolds.

I dare you to put the question to God! It is a dare, because experience has taught me never to ask a question to which you might get an answer you don't want to hear... But there will be an answer, and an adventure. I hope and pray that, as you read this book and follow the suggestions for reflection and action it contains, it will help you to hear the answer and to fulfil the adventure.

SECTION 1

WHAT WILL YOU DO WITH YOUR LIFE?

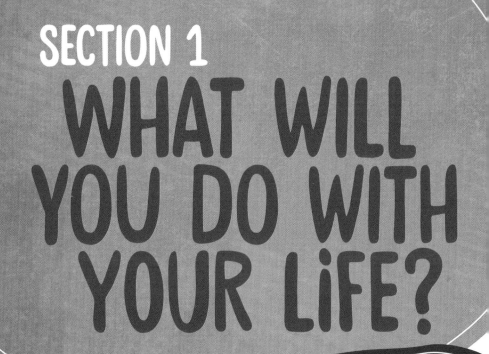

There are two great days in a person's life – the day we are born and the day we discover why.

WILLIAM BARCLAY

Seeking God's plan

Jesus' life, death and resurrection reshape history. Believing in him changes everything! Jesus gives us a radical new understanding of the world.

What it means to be human is redefined in the moment that we are baptized. Each of us is made in God's image to reflect his glory and bring about the flourishing of all creation. Our decision to follow Jesus and to become more like him will underpin every subsequent choice we make.

Whether you are pondering a new job, a new place to live, a sense of calling to serve God or a particular role at church or on the mission field, **Life is for Giving** will help you reflect on who you are, who God is calling you to be and what impact he is inviting you to have in his world. It will help you answer the question: **What will I do with my life?** In church we often use King David's words:

> For all things come from you,
> and of your own have we given you.
> **1 Chronicles 29.14**

As believers, we know that God has given us our lives and that we are called to give them back.

Choosing what to give our life to can be a complex and difficult decision. Today, we are often overwhelmed with choice. From coffee shops to the Internet, we are bombarded with options. Our decisions are instinctively influenced by a number of factors: our past experiences, our present situation, our unconscious habits, and who is with us at the time. While few of us seek God's opinion when choosing between a flat white and an espresso, when we seek God's plan for our lives we long to hear his voice saying, 'Walk this way'.

Life is for Giving will help you hear God's voice speaking through your history, your present reality, your identity and the community you are a part of. It will help you uncover ways in which God is already shaping you, and open you to hear his voice speaking directly to your heart.

The still small voice

In 1 Kings 19, Elijah the prophet is on the run. His life is in a mess, and he is desperate to know where God would take him next. He longs for God to speak, expecting a spectacular earthquake or fire, but eventually hears God in what the Bible calls the 'still small voice' (KJV) of a gentle breeze. Learning to listen to God – in whatever form his voice comes – is what you need to do in order to discern God's call on your life. And, because God can use just about anything to speak to us, we're going to look at how God's calling might be evident in and through five different areas: **history, reality, identity, community** and **divinity.**

As we review our **history** – the experiences and decisions that have brought us to where we are today – we will see how God is forming us out of dust, drawing us along a unique route towards his goal, and transforming us by his Holy Spirit.

Our present **reality** will be the springboard to whatever comes next, so we will consider how to read it and review it.

God has made us all unique: our habits and personality reflect our **identity**. But as believers we are given a new identity in Jesus and then that is enriched by the work of the Holy Spirit.

Three key truths

As you seek God's plan you might want to hold on to three key truths:

- First, God calls each and every one of us, no matter where we are at – because God made each of us and God loves each of us, just as we are.

- Second, God can and does use just about anything to equip us and point us towards the adventure he has in store for us.

- Third, God's plan involves our future flourishing and fulfilment – redeeming the past, not limited by it.

Our church **community** know us through our talents, gifts and roles. We will reflect on how we fit in and how we can give that church family opportunities to speak into our lives and vocation.

The final sections of **Life is for Giving** will describe how we hear God's voice more directly, allowing his **divinity** to impact our lives more fundamentally.

One traditional invitation to confession includes these words: 'You that truly … intend to lead a new life … draw near with faith'. It invites us to be *intentional* and *faithful* in the way we face our future. **Life is for Giving** assumes you are coming to these questions faithfully and will help you focus your intentions. Wherever you are starting from, God is able to do amazing things through you.

Reflect

[God] is able to accomplish abundantly more than all we can ask or imagine. **Ephesians 3.20**

Take my life, and let it be
Consecrated, Lord, to Thee;
Take my moments and my days,
Let them flow in ceaseless praise.

Frances Ridley Havergal

Act

Go for a quiet walk asking God to open your eyes, ears and heart – to be stretched so you might begin to imagine all that he longs to do through you.

SECTION 2

HiSTORY FORMING US

How did I get here?

Many of us have asked David Byrne's question: 'How did I get here?' As you seek God's plan for your life, it's a really great question to start with.

> For you created my inmost being; you knit me together in my mother's womb. I praise you because I am fearfully and wonderfully made.
> **Psalm 139.13–14a (NIV)**

God wonderfully knitted you together in the womb. Planned or unplanned, whether you were conceived in love, by accident or scientific feat, it was God who made you. You bear his fingerprint, a heavenly hallmark, and you are made for eternity.

There are over seven billion people on the planet, each uniquely made by God. Seven billion bricklayers, preachers or sous chefs would not be a smart way to build the world, develop society or establish a church. The fact that I am not like you and you are not like the person next to you is all part of God's master-plan. You are made to reflect God's glory through the particular combination of circumstances and opportunities he sends your way. That's the premise of Psalm 139.

Nobody is an accident or unwanted, however they came into the world – don't let anyone define you in that way.

From before you were born you were created the way you are because God wanted one like you! Nick Vujicic, author and motivational speaker (born with a rare disorder, with no legs or arms), says: 'I know for certain God does not make mistakes, but he does make miracles, I am one, you are too.'

Your life is a series of particular experiences, relationships and decisions unmatched by any other person on the planet. God does not want to waste anything you have been through; good or bad, enjoyable or scary, but to use it to form you for his glory. In Romans, Paul says:

> We know that all things work together for good for those who love God, who are called according to his purpose.
> **Romans 8.28**

Your history

Where you were born, your early childhood experiences, your natural skills, the passions formed during your formative years; all these things God will work with to shape you into the person he wants you to become.

Philippa's story

Philippa was hugely disappointed when what she had thought to be a 'dream' vocation was denied her in her late twenties. As she turned her story over to God she saw more and more of God's hand in her history and realized, rather, that he had been equipping her for something quite different. The 'no' to one thing was, in reality, a divine 'yes' to something else. She has since spent many fulfilling years in a role she had not previously imagined: running doctors' surgeries and establishing a Christian counselling charity.

Your history starts with your physical attributes, natural talents and earliest relationships; over time you have developed habits, hobbies, learning and interests. All of this God will use to form you if you let him. Your history is uniquely yours, and is unchangeable. As you look back over your life with a renewed curiosity, asking God to reveal aspects you have forgotten, you may see things differently and patterns may emerge. Reflecting on, dealing with, and owning your history will free you to celebrate who you are today and prepare you to grasp the future.

Pray

I am not one in a crowd for God, I am not a serialized number nor a catalogued card; I am unrepeatably unique, for God calls me by name. This reality I may certainly characterize as my personal identity, or my personal orientation in life, or my most profound and true self. Biblically, however, I prefer to call it my personal vocation.

Herbert Alphonso

Almighty God, help me to recognize the particular gifts you have given me, and to use them to fulfil your plan for my life. Amen.

Act

1. Draw a timeline of your life, noting significant life events and special moments where God has been particularly present, blessing you or revealing his will.

2. Map your birth family and other significant relationships. (This is sometimes called a Genogram.) Consider how each person has impacted your life or left you examples for good or for bad.

And all of us, with unveiled faces, seeing the glory of the Lord as though reflected in a mirror, are being transformed into the same image from one degree of glory to another; for this comes from the Lord, the Spirit.

2 CORINTHIANS 3.18

SECTION 3

HiSTORY
TRANSFORMING US

Facing forwards, not backwards

When we become Christians, we enter into Jesus' worldwide family, and God's Holy Spirit starts transforming us to become more like Jesus. This means that we're no longer defined by our past failures but by Jesus' forgiveness and future reign. We can begin to face forwards, not backwards!

Your past probably includes things you are now ashamed of or embarrassed by, things that you thought, said or did that you know God wouldn't be pleased with. Perhaps others have done things to you that have also left you embarrassed or ashamed. The good news is that when Jesus died on the cross, he dealt with all the sin and brokenness of the world. His death and resurrection, his love, his grace and his Holy Spirit are freely available to you. God wants to transform you from one degree of glory to another (2 Corinthians 3.18). Jesus' death and resurrection offer hope in a broken world and a new life unconstrained by the shortcomings of our past. Your history does not define your destiny.

God's values, God's purposes

Stepping into God's family, we are increasingly defined by the traditions, values and habits of God's kingdom. Paul writes to a church of young Christians:

Do not be conformed to this world, but be transformed by the renewing of your minds
Romans 12.2

If we allow God repeatedly to renew our minds, we will increasingly become the people he wants us to be. For some of us, this might be enhanced through counselling, mentoring or prayer. Jesus' promise of abundant life in John 10 requires us to immerse ourselves in that new life. As we do so, he refines us and we increasingly perceive his purposes being worked out in our daily lives, right where we are.

God has given you new perspective and understanding, new responsibilities and relationships since you began following Jesus. He may have granted you spiritual gifts. All this is transforming you:

Biblical transformations

There are many stories in the Bible of people transformed by God over the course of their lives. Moses, David and Paul all committed murder, yet went on to become great leaders for God. Sarah, Rebekah, Hannah and Elizabeth were all childless long into adulthood before they each gave birth to children whom God used in hugely significant ways. Both Simeon and Anna had lived almost a full lifetime when they experienced their most significant encounter with God, meeting the infant Jesus in the Temple (Luke 2).

... for it is God who is at work in you, enabling you both to will and to work for his good pleasure.
Philippians 2.13

14

> There is a crack in everything
> That's how the light gets in
> LEONARD COHEN, ANTHEM

God's great plan of grace is seen in the way he redeems the negative aspects of our past, literally restoring us and transforming us by the power of his Holy Spirit.

We need to own our past and simultaneously welcome God's transforming love in our lives. I recall some sage advice in a pastoral tweet I once received: 'Occasionally, weep deeply over the life you hoped would be, grieve the losses. Then wash your face, trust God and embrace the life you have.'

You are already so much more than your history, and you have more potential than you can possibly imagine.

Reflect

Past put behind us, for the future take us,
Lord of our lives, to live for Christ alone.

Timothy Dudley-Smith

Act

1. Give thanks for all that God has done with you since you chose to follow Christ: the new friendships, opportunities, freedom, insights and joy he has given you.
2. Offer to God those parts of your history that burden you, and those parts of your life still broken, seeking his forgiveness, freedom and grace.

SECTION 4
READING OUR REALITY

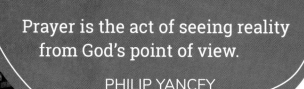

God's point of view

How might God view your current situation? God has allowed you to arrive where you are now, in a certain place among particular people who are all themselves going through specific stages of their lives.

The God who knows the hairs on your head and owns the cattle on a thousand hills has a purpose for you in your here and now. Your current reality will shape you for whatever is next – because God meets us where we are and wastes nothing. Your task is to read and explore your present reality, and so to see it as God sees it.

Place

Paul wrote many New Testament letters while literally 'in chains' in prison. He took every opportunity, good or bad, to fulfil God's purpose. From the day he met Jesus, Paul began to preach, teach and write about the good news, whenever and wherever he could. What are your opportunities where you are now?

People

God may call us to places or God's calling may be about particular people. The Church is sent to make disciples of all nations, so we serve the people God puts us alongside. One young woman I know believed God was calling her to India, until he showed her afresh the Bangladeshi crowds of her East London neighbourhood. She realized it was time to stop chasing a faraway dream and start living it right where she already was. How might God fulfil your passion right where you are, opening your eyes to glimpse God's image in those around you as well as to realize your own blind spots?

Seasons

Ecclesiastes 3 describes 'seasons' in our lives as times of healing, crying, building, dancing, mending and so on. These might correlate thematically with significant life events such as bereavement, surgery, or a new job. On the other hand, Shakespeare describes 'seven ages of man' moving chronologically from youth through to old age. Whatever your age and stage – your season – this will inform and affect what you can do and where you can go for God. Some seasons will need all your effort and concentration to survive before you can even consider moving on. Other seasons may make you restless and curious about your future.

Georgina's map

One evening Georgina set up a mapping event for our church family, where we each mapped our daily lives, the routes from home to work, our social settings and recreational routes. We noticed afresh the shops, estates and public buildings we passed, the people and their stories that made up our days. It led us to pray for them differently, and some of us began to make personal connections we never would have without stopping to look around us.

A common challenge for all of us is to live 'in the moment' while also realizing that we don't have to do everything in the next 18 months. Our energy level, health and financial abilities, the presence or otherwise of dependants will all rise and fall throughout our lifetime. Leaving something until later simply gives us more time to enjoy the present and prepare for it, so long as we are clear that we're not procrastinating. Equally, some opportunities may not reoccur, in which case it may be timely to seize them!

Pray

I am no longer my own but yours.
Put me to what you will, rank me with whom you will;
put me to doing, put me to suffering;
let me be employed for you, or laid aside for you, exalted for you,
or brought low for you; let me be full, let me be empty,
let me have all things, let me have nothing:
I freely and wholeheartedly yield
all things to your pleasure and disposal.
And now, glorious and blessed
God, Father, Son and Holy Spirit, you are mine and
I am yours. So be it. And the covenant
now made on earth, let it be ratified in heaven.

Methodist Covenant prayer

Act

Take a journal, and record, using words, pictures,
poetry or prayers, where you are right now, who
you are among and what season of life you are in.
It will help you see your reality from God's point of
view, and over time you will begin to see patterns
emerge. Write anything down that you think God is
drawing your attention to right now.

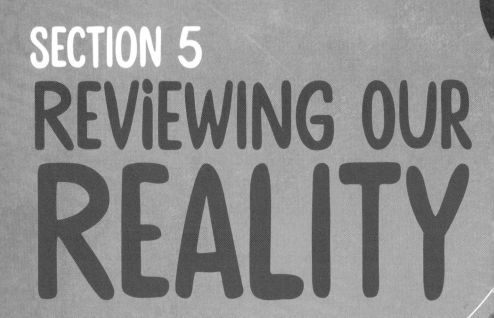

SECTION 5
REVIEWING OUR REALITY

> Life can only be understood backwards but it must be lived forwards.
>
> SØREN KIERKEGAARD

Living forwards

I remember my spiritual director telling me that God is always preparing us in the present for what our future holds. In his divine economy, God doesn't like to waste any opportunity to invest in our lives.

Augustine of Hippo says that we should **'trust the past to God's mercy, the present to his love and the future to his providence'**.

This section of **Life is for Giving** offers a very simple way for you to reflect on your present situation so that you can invest what you discover into your future. If you want to follow God's purposes, then having read and understood your current reality you need to develop a pattern of reviewing it.

Examen

One long-established prayer practice helps us review what is happening in our lives, turning our daily circumstances over to God for celebration or repair. Ignatian spirituality incorporates the practice of the examen. This is most simply a coming before God at the end of the day to review with him what has gone well and what has not gone well. Over the course of most days there are times when he has seemed close and we have felt in accord with his will and there are times when he has felt distant and we have said or done things outside of his will. For the good moments when he has seemed close, we thank him. For those not so good moments when we have strayed or felt out of touch with God, we seek his healing and forgiveness, asking for the strength of his Holy Spirit to guide us tomorrow more frequently into the orbit of his love and purpose.

Consolation and desolation

Ignatian spirituality also suggests that our lives move between consolation, when God feels close and all seems well, and desolation, when he doesn't and life feels barren. Doing an examen regularly will help you identify the patterns you most often inhabit. Consolation will give you a healthy focus beyond yourself; good bonds with your community; an ability to see the joys and sorrows of others; a refreshed inner vision; and renewed energy. Desolation will leave you falling into negative thought patterns; cutting yourself off from community; losing your landmarks; and becoming drained of energy.

Making decisions

Doing an examen regularly, especially if you share what you discover with a prayer partner or a spiritual director, will help you choose patterns that lead more frequently into times of consolation. Ignatius teaches that times of consolation are good for making big decisions, while big decisions are not best made in times of desolation. He also teaches that we should not in times of desolation abandon decisions made in consolation.

A rule of life

You may like to write down a simple set of precepts and patterns that you will seek to live by that incorporate the examen. These will help you choose to live in ways that more frequently move you into times of consolation.

Let your delight be in the Lord,
and he will give you your heart's desire.
Psalm 37.4

When you set time aside to enjoy God through this kind of prayerful attentiveness, God can literally shape your desires and help you to become more aware of how he is growing you to be more like Jesus.

Pray

Here is my heart, O God; here it is with all its secrets.
Look into my thoughts, O my hope, and take away all my wrong feelings.
Let my eyes be ever on you and release my feet from the snare.
I ask you to live with me, to reign in me, to make this heart of mine
a holy temple, a fit dwelling for your divine majesty.

Augustine of Hippo

Act

Practise tonight doing an examen of today, by asking yourself two questions:

1. What has given me life today and when have I felt close to God?
2. What has taken life from me today and when have I felt far from God?

Give thanks for the first and then seek God's grace and forgiveness for the second. Then ask God for his Spirit to lead you tomorrow more often to choose life and to stay close to him.

You might want to download an app or a podcast that includes an examen-style reflection, such as Pray As You Go (**www.pray-as-you-go.org**), to help you.

SECTION 6
OUR IDENTITY IN JESUS

> The Bible says that our real problem is that every one of us is building our identity on something besides Jesus.
>
> TIM KELLER

A new creation

The Bible is unequivocal:

> If anyone is in Christ, there is a new creation: everything old has passed away; see, everything has become new!
> **2 Corinthians 5.17**

As we submerge our lives into the presence of Jesus and invite him to live within us, our very identity is redefined. Our new identity is most significantly defined by Jesus' death, his resurrection and the sending of his Holy Spirit into our lives. The Church teaches that we have died with Jesus, that we are raised with him and that by the work of his Holy Spirit we are inwardly renewed and sanctification has begun.

There are a number of aspects to this new identity. Here we will explore just four of them that will form the basis of our discipleship. As we push into each of them, they will enrich our lives and help us to worship and serve our heavenly Father.

Children

Jesus teaches us to pray 'Our Father'. On the cross he looks at John and says to his own mother, 'Here is your son,' while to John he says, 'This is your mother' (John 19.27), and with that he inaugurates the eternal family of the Church. Furthermore, Paul in Romans teaches that through Jesus' gracious redemption we are each adopted as sons and daughters of the living God (Romans 8). This new status offers a privilege and intimacy that is ours for the rest of our life:

we freely receive the incredible privilege whereby we can call the creator 'Abba, Father'. We are literally made the brothers and sisters of Jesus himself.

Followers

A new interest in 'leadership' is seeing more entrepreneurial and ambitious character traits among those being ordained. But 'leaders' have led God's people since Abraham. Time and again, what makes a leader of God's people effective is their primary commitment to be followers. Jesus called the disciples to 'Follow me' (Mark 1.17). It would be three years before he commissioned them for leadership. 'Follow me' was – and is – the original invitation. In following Jesus, we follow his dreams, visions, words and passions. You may be a pioneer, a leader, a role model, an innovator or an entrepreneur, but before everything else you are called to be a follower of Jesus.

'The purpose of our life is God's glory. However lowly a life is, that is what makes it great.'

OSCAR ROMERO

'You are a priest at the wheel, my friend, if you work with honesty, consecrating that taxi of yours to God, bearing a message of peace and love to the passengers who ride in your cab.'

OSCAR ROMERO

Servants

... the Son of Man came not to be served but to serve, and to give his life a ransom for many.
Matthew 20.28

All Christian vocation has its roots in the bowl of water with which Jesus washed his disciples' feet the night before he gave his life on the cross. At this point, he tells us to do for each other as he has done for us (John 13.14–15).

God gives us our lives and the pattern of discipleship is found in giving them back to him and to his world. This is living as a servant of God and it is a costly privilege.

Ambassadors

In the closing verses of Matthew's Gospel, Jesus is recorded sending his first disciples to make disciples of all nations. Other Gospels record him telling them to be his witnesses to the world. Paul, just three verses after describing Christians as 'a new creation', asserts in 2 Corinthians 5.20 that they are also therefore ambassadors of Christ himself. So we are sent to witness to his love and his kingdom – ambassadors not because we have achieved or earned this absurd responsibility through years of hard work, study or back-slapping, but because God freely bestows it upon us. At the moment we put our trust into Jesus, he sends us as ambassadors, diplomats and emissaries of heaven itself.

> Expect great things from God, attempt great things for God.
>
> **WILLIAM CAREY**

Reflect

Where are you? All of us are called to grow continually into these four aspects of our identity. Sometimes we get stuck in one of them: as children, not growing out of an immature faith; as followers, desperately trying to learn everything before serving. Some are so busy being servants they miss out on the Father's loving touch, while others live only as ambassadors, slow to serve, unwilling to learn and often prone to pride.
Which aspect do you most easily identify with?
Which aspect do you see a need to grow in?

> To the church of God in Corinth, to those sanctified in Christ Jesus and called to be his holy people
>
> 1 CORINTHIANS 1.2 (NIV)

OUR IDENTITY IN THE HOLY SPIRIT

A holy people

Paul says to the young Corinthian church that Christians are primarily called to be 'a holy people'. To be holy is to reflect God's character, God's nature – to mirror the beauty of God's holiness in our lives.

For all of us today, whatever our specific callings, whether to nursing, engineering, banking, mission, acting or deep-sea exploration, there is a more fundamental calling: to be holy, as God is holy.

> Ministry is not what you do but who you are.
>
> BILL JOHNSON

Once we have put our trust in Jesus, the Holy Spirit begins to work in us. In the confirmation service, the Church prays over the newly confirmed that they would daily increase in the Holy Spirit. This is about the process of being formed and empowered to live into God's likeness.

The fruit of the Spirit

As our life becomes increasingly animated by God's Holy Spirit, others will see the fruit of the Spirit's presence, as described in Galatians 5:

> ... love, joy, peace, patience, kindness, generosity, faithfulness, gentleness, and self-control.
> **Galatians 5.22–23**

We might understand this list as the outworking of God's character of holiness in its earthly human features. It is this fundamental character of holiness – as people distinctively shaped by the Holy Spirit – that the Church regards as foundational in those appointed to formal ministries according to the traditional threefold order: that is, through ordination as deacons, priests and bishops.

There is further outworking of the gifts of the Spirit in the New Testament, for example in Ephesians 4. On a functional level, these gifts can be interpreted as suggesting five different 'modes' in ministry: apostolic, prophetic, evangelistic, pastoral and teaching (Ephesians 4.11).

This analysis usefully prompts us to ask not only, 'How do I reflect God's character of holiness in who I *am*?' but also, 'How do my gifts suggest what I might most suitably *do* in ministry?' Another way of putting this is to say that discerning God's call is about both grace and gifts: it involves on the one hand exploring the impact of God's grace on me, and on the other exploring my gifts – charisms – and how they might impact others.

Apostolic

'Apostolic' references the twelve whom Jesus originally chose, first to follow and subsequently to lead. It requires conviction and boldness. Strong leadership gifts are evidenced in the capacity to inspire and encourage: to awaken dreams, to establish churches and to offer stability even amid storms. Through this distinctive kind of leadership, God's reign is extended on earth, and others come to glimpse the kingdom of heaven.

Prophetic

'Prophetic' refers to those who speak out for God, no matter how unwelcome or unpopular the word they deliver. They tend to have remarkable courage as well as a deep capacity for discerning God's voice and God's will. They may deliver it orally or in writing, to people individually or collectively, in word or in deed. They are typically more concerned for God's glory than for their own comfort.

Evangelistic

'Evangelistic' relates to those who are gifted and empowered to make the truth of Jesus known to those they are in contact with. They are carriers of good news and often can't help bubbling over with it. If you are an evangelist, you will stir in others a curiosity and desire to know Jesus and you will love inviting them to join God's family.

Pastoral

'Pastoral' people long to help individuals, relationships and communities flourish. They create safe environments for people to explore life and take risks, to find healing and wholeness. If you are a pastor, you will probably already be at the heart of your church family, someone on whom others depend for care and encouragement in living towards their God-given purposes.

Teaching

The 'teaching' mode describes those who love to make the truth about God accessible to all. They like to break down confusion and help others find clarity about who God is, what God has done and how he intends for the world and the Church to be. They are effective communicators who empower others through the sharing of wisdom.

All the gifts of the Spirit are given for the building up of the Church, because the Spirit's work includes guiding us in truth and bonding us in unity (John 14.17). Fundamentally, this is the purpose of all ministry – to build up the body so that God's people are indeed God's holy people, empowered and enabled together to reach out to the world with the beauty of God's holiness. Exploring this model is a great way to see how God's Spirit has started to be at work within your life.

Reflect

Defend, O Lord, these your servants with your heavenly grace, that they may continue yours for ever, **and daily increase in your Holy Spirit** more and more until they come to your everlasting kingdom. Amen.

From the Common Worship Confirmation Service

Act

What might be your charisms, the gifts given you by the Spirit? Spend some time meditating further on the fruits of the Spirit in Galatians 5.22–23 and on the fivefold ministries described in Ephesians 4.7–13. For a tool that might help you in this process, see: **www.fivefoldministry.com**

SECTION 8
SERVING OUR COMMUNITY

> Christians are not naturally born ...
> Christians are intentionally made
> by an adventuresome church
>
> STANLEY HAUERWAS

'Resident aliens'

As part of a local church, you belong to a church family through baptism, and you are part of a community that is tasked with a mission.

This and the next section of **Life is for Giving** are about recognizing our place within the body of Christ, and thus listening to God's voice in and through the community in which we find ourselves. It is a context in which the whole is greater than the sum of the parts – and thus a great lens through which to understand how God might be shaping you for the future.

Stanley Hauerwas' book **Resident Aliens** concerns the reality that Christians while on earth are in fact citizens of heaven. As a 'resident alien' you are charged with imparting the values and message of heaven to planet earth. You are not called to do this alone, but as part of a community of sinners-becoming-saints with whom your impact is manifested and magnified. Whether you are on the leadership team or a service rota, or simply welcoming the person in the seat next to you, you can make a remarkable difference. With and through the church family – no matter how big or small, how exciting or how struggling – God is at work transforming the world. It is a wonder, but as with flakey disciples so also with fallible churches, God chooses to fulfil his work in the world through his people.

A missional Church

Peter writes to the dispersed Church towards the end of the first century that they are still:

> ... a chosen people, a royal priesthood, a holy nation, God's special possession, that you may declare the praises of him who called you out of darkness into his wonderful light.
> **1 Peter 2.9 (NIV)**

Four amazing and complementary descriptions of the Church and one unmistakable reason for its existence: to declare the praise of God, who brings light out of darkness and hope out of despair.

These four collective descriptions work as a counterpoint to what we read in Section 6 about our personal identity in Jesus. Peter makes clear to his readers then and now that they are only fully themselves when they are part of a missional Church that is seeking to give away the life it has been given by God. Each description takes us further in understanding how we might serve the Church:

A chosen people

As a chosen people we stand in the tradition of Israel: chosen out of the nations to be a light to the nations. Inaugurated at Pentecost, we are an eschatological family called to live a covenant relationship with God and for God, for the world to see and be drawn to.

A royal priesthood

As one of the royal priesthood we are redeemed for ministry. Karl Barth said that our baptism is not just into the life of the Church but specifically into the ministry of the Church. We are all called to be priests who mediate heaven to earth and offer earth to heaven.

A holy nation

A member of the holy nation will reflect the holiness of God, living with others in a gathered community of followers who have been bound together by an identity that is stronger, deeper and longer lasting than any terrestrial nationality.

God's own possession

As one of God's special possessions we know ourselves as precious and loved, not just for our personal comfort and privilege, though that is part of it; we are treasured that we may declare his praises. His love and our privilege move us to serve him and his Church.

Being part of the body of Christ

Paul describes the Church a number of times as the body of Christ, each of us members or parts of that body with unique and critical functions to perform if the Church is going to be a coordinated, beautiful and effective body.

> ... we must grow up in every way into him who is the head, into Christ, from whom the whole body, joined and knitted together by every ligament with which it is equipped, as each part is working properly, promotes the body's growth in building itself up in love.
>
> **Ephesians 4.15–16**

Like a human body, we are growing and maturing and developing. What part do you currently play in the life of your church? What skills, natural talents and spiritual gifts are you exercising in the life of the church? Do you naturally encourage, explain, complain, or see better ways to do things? Maybe you are the one who spots the newest person in church, or goes out of your way to talk to more vulnerable members of the church community. This is you being part of the body of Christ; this is you serving the community.

Pray

Eternal God and Father, you create and redeem us by the power of your love: guide and strengthen us by your Spirit, that we may give ourselves in love and service to one another and to you; through Jesus Christ our Lord.

The Collect for Tuesday Morning Prayer, Common Worship

Act

Observe the various relationships you have been given and the roles you inhabit in your church community.

1. What are the functions you have in the body?

2. Where do you fit into the relationships of the family?

3. How are you currently impacting the kingdom of God through belonging to the community of disciples?

SECTION 9
HEARING OUR COMMUNITY

No man is an island,
entire of itself; every man
is a piece of the continent,
a part of the main.

JOHN DONNE

A new society

We have the greatest technological connectivity our planet has ever seen, yet the individualization of western society is increasingly threatening the very social fabric of our world. We are in danger of becoming invisible to each other.

This, however, is exactly where the Church is good news. For 'the Church' is a new society offering people a community gathered around the vision and values of God's kingdom, a community in which each can know and be known by others. At its best, a church community is a safe place for transparent living and risky giving, supported by and committed to the mutual flourishing of all its members.

Shining his light in the world

Too few of us trust God – or our friends – enough to let God speak freely through them into our lives. Yet God established the Church as an *ecclesia* or 'gathering' and it is still his will that the Church nurtures and nourishes its members to shine his light in the world. A natural impulse of a healthy church community is to speak truth and to shine light into each other's lives. You don't need to discern God's will as an individualized island; indeed you can't. It takes the whole Church to hear the whole word of God. Thus, listening to your community will be key for hearing God's voice in your life. If your sense of a call is not corroborated by your church community, then it may just be your call and not God's call on your life.

The Bible suggests the testimony of two to three witnesses gives greater validity to what we discern to be of God. There are three common ways to hear God speaking to you through the Church: through **elders**, through **peers** and in the **incidental** conversations that take place every week.

Elders

You could seek out wisdom from an elder, a leader, a clergy or PCC member who will have the wisdom of years and some given authority with which to reflect on your gifts and ministry. Some in your church will have seen people like you before, and prayed long ago with those who now lead ministries, missions and churches elsewhere. Inviting them to respond as you explore and test out your gifts, calling and ministry is part of being church together.

Peers

Jesus says that where two or three of his followers come together in his name he will always be present among them. Seek to keep close company with such people where you can search out each other's hearts, voice your weaknesses as well as strengths, and trust them with your vulnerability. Pray with them – so that God is regularly part of the conversation circle. Ask them to challenge habits and hang-ups, as well as shape your dreams and desires. Who do they see you becoming?

Incidents

When you are fervently seeking God's direction, take note of 'incidental' things: a conversation containing the unexpected; something that strikes a chord; the divine nudge. Don't ignore it. Rather, ask what prompted it; explain why it seems significant and open the ears of your heart the wider to hear what God may be saying.

It is just possible that you have no real idea just how significant you are to the life of your church. Sunday school teachers have left lifelong marks on those they discipled as infants. Extroverts have sometimes unknowingly brought joy to church events and welcomed strangers into the family. Ask others what they see and value in you! An individualized process of discernment will always be poorer than one conducted among the fellowship of believers. And then ask the elders and your equals to pray for you, maybe using Paul's prayer in Ephesians 1.

Pray

I do not cease to give thanks for you as I remember you in my prayers. I pray that the God of our Lord Jesus Christ, the Father of glory, may give you a Spirit of wisdom and revelation as you come to know him, so that, with the eyes of your heart enlightened, you may know what is the hope to which he has called you, what are the riches of his glorious inheritance among the saints, and what is the immeasurable greatness of his power for us who believe, according to the working of his great power.

Ephesians 1.16–19

Act

1. Ask the elders at your church to reflect back to you both your gifts and your gaps.
2. Invite your peers for a drink and dare to share your hopes and dreams.
3. Listen for and make a note of the incidental wisdom that comes your way.
4. Ask your church community to pray for you, listening for God's answers.

SECTION 10
DiViNiTY
HOW GOD SPEAKS

God called to Moses out of the bush, 'Moses, Moses! ... Come no closer! Remove the sandals from your feet, for the place on which you are standing is holy ground.'

EXODUS 3.4–5

The voice of God

God chatted with Adam in the garden, told Noah to build an ark and Abraham to look at the stars. God spoke to Rebekah about the children in her womb, to Lydia by the river and to Moses from out of a burning bush! The Father told Jesus he was pleased with him and Paul heard Jesus' voice on the way to Damascus. Just how does God speak today?

Life is for Giving has explored various aspects of our lives through which God might speak. This section is about seeking the voice of God directly. You may hear God speak to you in ways he has done before, but equally he may choose to speak a new thing to you in a new way. Open yourself up to listen deeply, ponder slowly and then test your hearing carefully! The following are some of the chief ways in which God's voice has been heard in the past.

God speaks through his word

The Bible is described as God's word, sharper than a two-edged sword, able to get between our deepest thoughts and feelings (Hebrews 4.12). God has consistently chosen to reveal himself to the world through his 'word'. Paul tells Timothy that the Bible is God-breathed and will equip God's servants for every good work (2 Timothy 3.16–17). Reading, studying, meditating on and hearing the Bible taught will position you to hear God giving both general direction to your life and calling, forming, challenging and encouraging you more specifically along the way. God doesn't contradict himself, so God's word also gives you a tool with which to measure all the specific things you think he might be saying.

God speaks through his Son

The 'Word' became flesh and dwelt among us: Jesus is the ultimate revelation of God, the exact representation of God's being, the radiance of his glory. The Gospels are therefore a special repository within scripture revealing God incarnate and his passion for the world. The words uttered by Christ here and in God's revelation to John give you an especially intimate glimpse into the very heart of God. Speaking

41

personally, I have heard God's voice more often through the Gospels than in any other part of scripture, even though all scripture is God-breathed.

God speaks through his Spirit

On the day of Pentecost, Peter declared God's ancient promise to send the Holy Spirit on all his children. The young would see visions and the old would be given holy dreams. Throughout Acts and up to the present day, this is evidenced in action. The Holy Spirit still visits God's people, disclosing his will and his heart. Jesus said that the Holy Spirit would lead us into all truth. Peter heard the Spirit tell him to visit the house of Cornelius and take the good news to the gentiles. When you read the scriptures, when you pray quietly and wait on God, you can expect to hear God calling to you. The Holy Spirit never tires from wanting to press the Father's heart upon us.

God speaks through the Sacraments

Whenever we meet for worship it has the potential to be an encounter with the risen Christ. But Holy Communion, perhaps more than any other form of service, makes this transformation vivid and real. The Eucharist brings us directly into Christ's presence by a special kind of remembering that makes his Easter victory present to us. The bread and wine, ordinary food and drink, become charged with the memory of Christ's death and resurrection. You may hear God speak to you through the sacrament of Holy Communion as you draw near to God, and God draws near to you. Sometimes you won't be able to explain it in words. At their core, sacraments are outward and visible signs of God's inward and invisible grace.

God speaks through his creation

Abraham heard God as he gazed at the stars, for God can make a flower bloom a week early, or a blackbird arrive as we pray. He can bring the sea to storm or the clouds to clear. And in a myriad of similar ways, God may choose to get your attention just as he did with Moses at the burning bush.

> Ever since the creation of the world his eternal power and divine nature, invisible though they are, have been understood and seen through the things he has made.
> **Romans 1.20**

Many people testify to hearing God, particularly outdoors, but I was standing in Digbeth bus station at 3am, fresh snow falling on the dark diesel-stained floor just beyond the entrance, when I heard his voice. From that moment I knew that Jesus made perfect sense and I have followed him ever since.

God speaks through his people

At the beginning of 1 Corinthians 14 Paul explains that God uses prophecy to strengthen, comfort and encourage his children. 'Words of knowledge' and 'prophetic utterances' may be given specifically to one believer for the benefit of another. When someone is praying with you or for you, God may speak words for you through them. It's amazing, but it's true. God loves you so much that he will use just about anyone and anything to impress his will upon your heart.

Reflect

Samuel called out in the middle of the night when he thought the Lord was near: 'Speak, for your servant is listening.'

1 Samuel 3.10

Act

1. Make a note of how God has spoken to you in the past.
2. Make a note of what God said.
3. Set aside an hour, a day or a few days to practise being quiet, open the Bible and listen for the still small voice of God.

> We often miss hearing God's voice simply because we aren't paying attention.
>
> RICK WARREN

SECTION 11
DiViNiTY
HOW WE HEAR

Paying attention

God is always more ready to speak than we are to listen. **Life is for Giving** is hopefully opening up ways for you to hear God's voice in different areas of your life. The more you respond, the more you will recognize the voice behind you that says:

> This is the way; walk in it.
> **Isaiah 30.21**

Below are ten key principles that have helped me over the years to hear God's voice.

1.	Get rid of the distractions, turn off the emails, find a quiet place, or go for a walk. 'Be still, and know that I am God.' **Psalm 46.10**

2.	Start with confession. Tell God how your life has drifted from his desires and yours. Repent and believe, turn and trust. Let God know you are back. **1 John 1.6-10**

3. Read God's word. Don't rush: meditate on it as a cow chews grass until every last bit of goodness is extracted. **Psalm 119.105**

4. When you pray, be slow to speak and quick to listen. God knows the thoughts of your heart. You barely know the depths of his. **James 1.19**

5. Open your heart during times of corporate worship when others are lifting their hearts to God in scripture and in song. Picture his Spirit dancing among the faithful. **John 4.24**

6. Open your ears to the fellowship of believers you belong to – one of them may have a message for you from God. **Matthew 18.20**

7. Write in a journal what you hear, your questions, prayers, pictures and answers. Note your relationship with God and return to it often. From Moses **(Exodus 17)** to John **(Revelation 21)** God says, 'Write it down.'

8. Weigh what you hear over weeks or months. Don't rush to give God a date by which you want a sign. Wait patiently and if it doesn't come, stay put, 'test everything'. **1 Thessalonians 5.16–22**

9. Practise living in the constant presence of God, always seeking to keep close to him, walking in step with his Spirit holding an ongoing conversation. **Matthew 10.25, 1 Thessalonians 5.16–18**

> Faith is taking the first step even when you don't see the whole staircase.
>
> MARTIN LUTHER

10. Grow your faith. To hear God on the big issues in your life, turn over to him the small things. If you want to hear God speaking into your earthly adventure, trust him and take faith steps every day on the heavenly adventure. Hearing is closely tied to obeying: the more closely you follow, the more fully you will enjoy God's fellowship and embrace his plans.

Don't let your own world become so loud you can't hear: for **'God makes himself most available to those who make themselves most available to him'**. In his book, **Hearing God**, Dallas Willard says that 'in our attempts to understand how God speaks to us and guides us we must, above all, hold on to the fact that learning how to hear God is to be sought only as a part of a certain kind of life, a life of loving fellowship with the King.' In other words, if you want to hear God, rather than simply straining to listen, you might lean into him in faith and trust. As you grow into a relationship of utter dependency, God's voice will likely grow more audible.

God trusts humanity with his creation, and trusts his children with his Church, so God will trust you with his dreams. Don't hold back. This heavenly Father wants as much of you to engage with as much of him as you can manage.

> Do all the good you can.
> By all the means you can.
> In all the ways you can.
> In all the places you can.
> At all the times you can.
> To all the people you can.
> As long as ever you can.
>
> **JOHN WESLEY**

Pray

Listen in silence, because if your heart is full of other things, you cannot hear the voice of God

Mother Teresa

Act

Try the ten principles in this section!

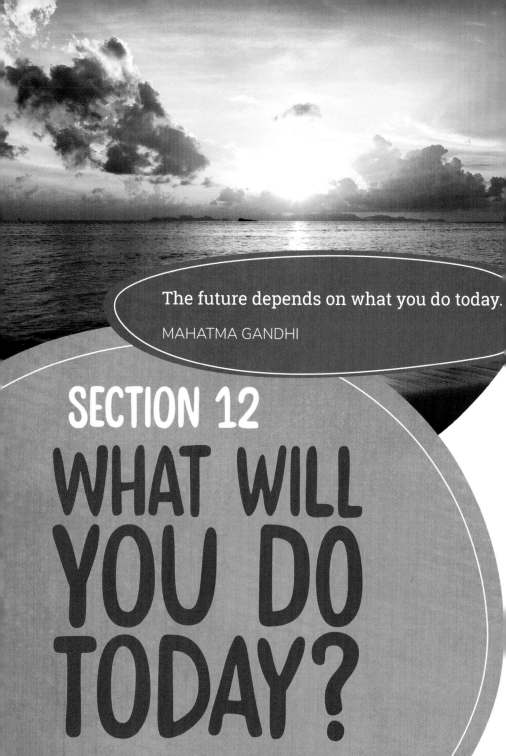

The future depends on what you do today.

MAHATMA GANDHI

SECTION 12

WHAT WILL YOU DO TODAY?

Choose life

In her Olympic song, Heather Small asked, 'What have you done today to make you feel proud?' But it's not just about today. What can you do today that your future self will be pleased you did?

And it's not a silly question: our tomorrows are shaped by the habits, conversations and decisions of today.

God has a plan for your life.

> For surely I know the plans I have for you,
> says the Lord, plans for your welfare and not for harm,
> to give you a future with hope.
> **Jeremiah 29.11**

God is calling you to step faithfully further into those plans – just as you began to do when you first chose to follow Jesus. Today God calls you to take another step.

Two callings

1. God calls all believers to love the Lord our God with all our heart (Deuteronomy 6.5); to be holy as God is holy (Leviticus 11.44); to act justly, love mercy and walk humbly with your God (Micah 6.8). Jesus echoes this general call to all who would follow, first to deny themselves and take up their cross (Matthew 16.24). And Paul underlines it with the words: 'Rejoice always, pray without ceasing, give thanks in all circumstances; for this is the will of God in Christ Jesus for you' (1 Thessalonians 5.16–18). All Christians have this foundational calling, and it is fundamental for any other.

> What we do with our days, we do with our lives.

2.   Our secondary calling is more specific: a call to each of us individually that relates to God's particular purpose for each and every life that is offered back to God. Discerning this calling is more complicated, so until it comes into focus, concentrate on living fully in God's general call. Hearing God's voice and following his direction are the most rewarding things you can do with your life, but can also be among the hardest!

In **Life is for Giving** we have explored five areas of your life through which you may perceive God's particular calling and equipping of your life:

Your history is a rich mine of experiences that have been forming you, and a series of encounters with God that have been transforming you.

Your present reality is shaping you at this very moment. It is the springboard into the rest of your life – so learn to read it and begin to review it, seeking God's presence in its midst.

Your identity as a child of God is sealed in Jesus Christ and in his Holy Spirit. You are loved beyond measure just because you are. Your credentials stem from deciding to trust Jesus and receiving the Holy Spirit.

> In whatever choices you have made, God is at no loss to perform his will concerning you.
>
> **AUGUSTINE OF HIPPO**

Your church community allows you to exercise your God-given gifts and graces. If you invite them to, other members will speak truth and challenge, encourage and help bring direction into your life.

Hearing the divine voice is utterly remarkable. Take every opportunity to listen for God, and remember, he can speak in a variety of ways.

Two lessons

Learn from those who found 'life is for giving' ahead of you. I love Jonah for what we learn from him.

1.   Jonah claims to have given himself to God, but in fact is found running away. He tries to ignore God's call to Nineveh and jumps on a boat to Tarshish instead – but it doesn't work. If God is calling, excuses don't work.

2. When a storm blows up and the sailors become convinced it is Jonah's fault, they ask: 'Where are you from? What do you do?' Jonah's answer, 'I am a Hebrew ... I worship the Lord' (Jonah 1.9), models for us how we might define ourselves: not by what we do but by who we are and who we worship.

God nudges Jonah to confess him as Lord, and Jonah asks the sailors to throw him overboard. Through this, God rescues Jonah and takes him on a divinely planned adventure.

Pray

My Lord God, I have no idea where I am going. I do not see the road ahead of me. I cannot know for certain where it will end. Nor do I really know myself, and the fact that I think that I am following your will does not mean that I am actually doing so. But I believe that the desire to please you does in fact please you. And I hope I have that desire in all that I am doing. I hope that I will never do anything apart from that desire. And I know that if I do this you will lead me by the right road though I may know nothing about it. Therefore will I trust you always though I may seem to be lost and in the shadow of death. I will not fear, for you are ever with me, and you will never leave me to face my perils alone.

Thomas Merton

Act

How would you answer the sailors:
'Where are you from?'
'What do you do?'

'Tell me, what is it you plan to do
With your one wild and precious life?'
Mary Oliver

Today we are often overwhelmed with choice. Whether you
are pondering a new job, a sense of calling or a particular role
at church, **Life is for Giving** is designed to help you answer the
question: What will I do with my life?

Life is for Giving contains twelve reflections which encourage you
to hear how God is calling you through your history, your present
reality, your identity and your community, opening yourself to hear
God's voice speaking directly to your heart. Each is accompanied
by actions to help you explore your vocation to the full.

Featuring practical exercises alongside material for prayer and
reflection, **Life is for Giving** is ideal for anyone exploring the next
step on their vocational journey.

Andy Rider is Rector of Christ Church Spitalfields. He has been a
minister for over 25 years, during which time he has helped many
discern God's purpose for their lives.

Also available from
Church House Publishing:

**The Great Vocations
Conversation**
A year of inspiration
and challenge
for ministers
ISBN 978 1 78140 095 1

ISBN: 978-1-78140-098-2

9 781781 400982

CHURCH HOUSE
PUBLISHING

www.chpublishing.co.uk